CHARISMA REPORTS: THE BROWNSVILLE REVIVAL

Charisma REPORTS

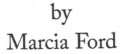

The Brownsville Revival

by
Marcia Ford

CREATION HOUSE
Orlando, FL

CHARISMA REPORTS: THE BROWNSVILLE REVIVAL by
Marcia Ford
Published by Creation House
Strang Communications Company
600 Rinehart Road
Lake Mary, Florida 32746
Web site: http://www.creationhouse.com

Copyright © 1997 by Creation House
All rights reserved
Printed in the United States of America
Library of Congress Catalog Card Number: 97-67239
ISBN: 0-88419-465-5
78901234 BBG 876543

First printing, May 1997
Second printing, June 1997

C ONTENTS

INTRODUCTION

IN EARLY 1994 the Holy Spirit visited a small church at the end of a runway near the Toronto airport in Mississauga, Ontario. You'd think that would make front-page news: Holy Spirit Descends on Believers in Canada!

Not quite. At the time, few in the media took notice of what was happening in any church anywhere. But *Charisma* magazine noticed. Freelance writer Daina Doucet— who would later work for Toronto Airport Christian Fellowship—was assigned to cover the story, and her article on what came to be known as the Toronto Blessing was the first to appear in an American magazine.

Eighteen months later and a thousand miles south of Toronto, revival broke out in Pensacola, Florida. Once again, *Charisma* magazine paid close attention. Within weeks, *Charisma* had a story in hand from Alice Crann, a reporter for the *Pensacola News-Journal. Charisma*'s first story about Pensacola appeared in "People and Events," the magazine's news section, in October of 1995.

Executive editor J. Lee Grady realized immediately that this revival was worth a feature article. Early in 1996 he spent several days in Pensacola, attending services, talking to visitors, and interviewing the staff at Brownsville Assembly of God. His feature story based on that trip appeared in the June 1996 issue.

Yet another follow-up story became necessary, as the revival showed no signs of waning. A second "People and Events" news story, cowritten by Grady and freelance writer Jim DeWitt, ran in *Charisma* in November 1996. Since then, Grady and many others from Strang Communications, the publisher of *Charisma,* have visited the Brownsville church to see for themselves what God is doing in northwestern Florida. What they, like so many others, have discovered is that this current move of God is stronger than ever.

Here is *Charisma*'s report on the phenomenon that has come to be known as the Brownsville Revival.

Marcia Ford
May 1997

1
THE
PANHANDLE
PROPHECY

THE SCENE COULD HARDLY have been more dramatic. Pastor David Yonggi Cho, known around the world as the leader of one of the most phenomenal church-growth movements in history, listened intently to the voice of the God he had served for so many decades.

The year was 1991, and a prophetic vision was unfolding before Cho's eyes. God began to speak to the South Korean pastor about a sweeping revival that would finally come to the United States, a nation that seemed to have been bypassed as God's Spirit flowed throughout other parts of the world.

At the Holy Spirit's prompting, Cho pulled out a map of America and allowed the Spirit to guide his hand to the area where this revival would break out.

His finger rested on Pensacola, a Florida panhandle city hardly associated with spiritual fervor. In fact, the city was known to the homosexual community as the "gay Riviera." A seven-mile stretch of beach on the Gulf of Mexico just east of the city attracted thousands of homosexuals and lesbians; over the Memorial Day weekend every year, the homosexual population reached as high as fifty thousand. Pensacola was definitely one place to be if you were gay.

It was also the place to be if you wanted an abortion. At one time, the city was home to three abortion clinics. Three clinic bombings on Christmas Eve of 1984 had put Pensacola on the map; within three years of Cho's vision, the murders of three clinic workers had drawn worldwide attention to the city of fifty-eight thousand people.

But on that night in 1991, Cho believed he had heard the voice of the Lord loud and clear: "I am going to send revival to the seaside city of Pensacola, and it will spread like a fire until all of America has been consumed by it." From Seattle, Washington, where Cho was conducting a meeting the night he received the vision, word spread across the country about the coming revival. In no time, it reached the ears of pastors in the Pensacola area.

And when Cho speaks, people listen.

Doubters believed news of the prophecy to be a rumor. Why would God speak to Dr. Cho, pastor of a church in Seoul with more than seven hundred thousand members, about a quiet Southern town that had never made any spiritual waves? But when Cho publicly confirmed that he had received the prophecy, leaders began to take the prophetic words seriously.

Among those leaders was John Kilpatrick, pastor of Brownsville Assembly of God in Pensacola. Once word of the prophecy reached Kilpatrick, he and his church's leadership set aside Sunday nights exclusively to pray for revival. For nearly three years, they prayed. They prayed for the lost, for political leaders, church leaders, denominational leaders, and school officials.

Several earlier and less-publicized prophecies also had indicated that the hand of God was pointing toward Pensacola. In 1979 Pastor Ken Sumrall, now retired, delivered a prophecy at Liberty Church, the nondenominational church he founded in Pensacola. It said of the coming revival: "Time will be forgotten as meetings will last for hours. . . . There will be much weeping and sobbing as sin is seen as exceedingly sinful. . . . Youth, even the very young, will be drunk with new wine and burn with fervor, oblivious to anything and everything but obedience to Jesus. . . . Prayer will be the main event of the church. Hundreds will be converted. Be prepared to baptize two hundred new believers at one service."

A second documented prophecy was given in Phoenix, Arizona, by Visionaries International leader Michial Ratliff. In November 1989 Ratliff prophesied:

> Transformation will come. Many people in peril, in dire straits, will be saved dramatically. Healings will take place. Deliverances will take place. And one church in particular will humble its heart and

receive Me. The college people, the students, the high schools, various people will be reckoned with by the angels of God that are loosed.

This is a victory against all contempt that is stirring in the city, actually disarming the time bomb that is ticking away in Pensacola, Florida. You shall see the turnaround, and nationally will the church hear about the revival that sparked in Pensacola.

Strong spiritual words for a city that seemed to produce nothing but bad news in the early nineties. The 1993 murder of abortionist Dr. David Gunn and the murders of abortion doctor John Britton and bodyguard James Barrett the following year had made the name of Pensacola synonymous with hatred, violence, and the media's favorite phrase of all, "right-winged, narrow-minded, fundamental Christianity."

Brownsville folks just dug in their heels and prayed even harder. If Satan thought he had a lock on this town, he was dead wrong.

By early 1995 the people of Pensacola apparently needed some reminders about the city's spiritual destiny. In February Jim Garlow, pastor of Skyline Wesleyan Church near San Diego, California, conducted special services at Pine Forest United Methodist Church and gave the congregation a prophetic word: "You will accomplish more in the next thirty-six months than you have in the last hundred years." For some that seemed unlikely, but those who had been faithfully praying for revival took Garlow's prophetic statement as though it came directly from God.

On May of 1995, as Christians gathered downtown to pray at a rally held in connection with the annual March for Jesus event, the crowd heard Cho's words again: "I am going to send revival to the seaside town of Pensacola. . . ."

For years, countless Christians in the area had hung onto the promise contained in those words. They had no trouble believing that promise was indeed from the Lord. The difficult part was the wait. How long would they have to wait? Their friends, neighbors, and family members were dying, suffering, sinning, wasting their lives. Where was the match that would ignite this fire that would be sparked in Pensacola and spread throughout America?

Brownsville Assembly continued praying, continued seeking the Father.

No one saw it coming. No one predicted the day and the hour. No one even suspected that the Father would come on the most obvious day of all—Father's Day.

2

A FOUNDATION OF FAITH

LONG BEFORE THE DAY that would change the course of so many lives, God prompted the congregation of Brownsville Assembly of God to abandon themselves to His will.

Nothing less would do. God knew what was in store for them. He knew that a time of unprecedented blessing awaited them—and He knew that nothing short of complete abandonment would see them through the often rough and rocky times of revival.

Not only did they need to submit themselves

to God but they also needed to commit themselves to each other.

For several years before the outbreak of revival, Brownsville's Sunday morning service included at least one element you're not likely to see in other Protestant churches—a weekly communion service. Kilpatrick would bless his congregation as the deacons blessed the pastoral staff during the communion portion of the service. That act alone went a long way toward creating a bond among the members of the church, as they found significance in a ritual often ignored in other congregations.

Dick Reuben, a messianic Jew who frequently leads the church's prayer services, is credited with lending a deep sense of spiritual significance to the communion service. Beginning in the early nineties, Reuben regularly taught on priesthood and communion and conducted what he called Golden Altar services. While no one can possibly know just what connection, if any, there is between this church's emphasis on communion and its later openness to revival, those who have been around since pre-revival days point to that emphasis as a definite factor in the maturing of the church.

Adding to that maturing process were the biblical teachings Reuben gave in which he used the Old Testament to shed light on the New Testament. Often when Reuben taught, the church would be transformed into the Tabernacle of Moses. By using reproductions of the priestly garments that would have been worn by Aaron and the furnishings that would have been found in the tabernacle, Reuben used tangible objects to help the people of Brownsville grow into their role as New Testament priests under the authority of Jesus, the High Priest.

But nothing laid the foundation for revival like prayer did. Years earlier, Kilpatrick spent an extended time in prayer about the direction the church's Sunday night services should take. During that time the Lord prompted him to turn to Matthew 21:13, which reads, "My house shall be called a house of prayer" (NKJV). In 1993 Kilpatrick and the church leadership decided to set the Sunday night service apart specifically for prayer, and the congregation soon caught the vision of a persistently praying church. Brownsville's road to revival was under construction.

Also "under construction" were the church's prayer banners—another evidence of this congregation's knack for bringing abstract concepts to life. As a continual reminder of the prayer needs of the church and the community, church members created a dozen different banners to help people focus on those areas they needed to bring before the Lord: warfare, family, lost souls, governmental leaders, healing, pastors, revival, schools, ministries, the peace of Jerusalem, children, and catastrophic events.

Leaders assigned to each banner would gather specific prayer requests related to the theme and lead prayer around the banner. After each banner focus was prayed about, the congregation would join in corporate prayer. And much to the surprise—and delight—of so many, the attendance at the Sunday evening prayer services began to increase.

"Prayer absolutely conditioned our church for revival," says Kilpatrick. For a reason they would not discover until two years later, a growing number of people found themselves particularly drawn to the revival banner, united in deep intercession.

Months before the revival began—again, during a time of intense prayer—Kilpatrick sensed the Holy Spirit telling him He was going to change his ministry, and He asked the pastor's permission to send someone to work with him.

"The Holy Spirit then gave me Ecclesiastes 4:9–10, which says, 'Two are better than one, because they have a good reward for their labor. For if they fall, one will lift up his companion. But woe to him who is alone when he falls, for he has no one to help him up'" (NKJV).

He didn't know it at the time but that man would be Stephen Hill, an evangelist from Texas. And together, they would have to figure out a way to work through the trying circumstances to come. As both men were about to learn, the glorious joy of true revival doesn't come without stirring up the hosts of hell, as the church threatens to destroy the demonic stranglehold on a city.

3

THE FATHER CHOOSES HIS DAY

IN ONE SENSE, the day Pastor John Kilpatrick's mother died signaled the very beginning of revival—though few people would have thought it at the time.

A month after her death, Kilpatrick found that he was far less able to handle his mother's passing than he had thought. She had died of cancer on May 7, and her illness and death had taken a tremendous toll on the then forty-five-year-old Kilpatrick. Before she died, Kilpatrick knew that revival was on its way. It was in the air, and its unmistakable scent was strong. Now, revival seemed far away.

Physically and emotionally drained, he called on Stephen Hill, a colleague in the Assemblies of God and a longtime friend, to preach at the evening service on Father's Day, June 18. The night before, Kilpatrick met with Steve and told him how grieved he was that so many people had left the church because of all his preaching on revival.

Kilpatrick was clearly still grieving over his mother's death as well. A gentle-natured man with a Georgia drawl, Kilpatrick admitted that he felt emotionless and even lacked the inspiration to prepare a sermon. He also asked Hill to preach at the morning service.

At first, nothing spectacular happened that Sunday morning. It was something of a typical worship service, except that maybe some minds were wandering a bit more than usual, planning meals and surprises and special presents for Dad.

As the clock struck noon, Hill gave an altar call. Suddenly, and unexpectedly, God came—and all heaven broke loose. A thousand people—half the people in the congregation—streamed forward to the altar for prayer.

At the same moment, Kilpatrick felt the sensation of wind blowing in the sanctuary. One person after another fell to the floor as Hill prayed for them. Others wept; some shook violently.

Hill prayed a simple prayer for Kilpatrick as he stood on the stage. "More, Lord," he said—and the pastor fell to the floor, where he lay for almost four hours. For the next forty-eight hours, Kilpatrick would be virtually useless to anyone but God Himself.

As the pastor lay on the floor, he felt a heavenly glory resting on him like a heavy blanket. God's presence was tangible at last.

"When I hit the floor, it felt like I weighed ten thousand pounds," Kilpatrick told *Charisma*. "I knew something supernatural was happening. God was visiting us."

That day, the morning service did not end until 4 P.M. And that night, the evening service didn't end until well after midnight. Revival had come.

In no time, word of the revival spread. People began lining up at 3 P.M. just to get a seat in the sanctuary, which at that time seated twenty-three hundred people. They'd stand in line, eating hamburgers from the local Burger King, or slices of pizza from Pizza Hut, which one night reportedly was forced to close early because the kitchen ran out of dough.

Inside the church, it became a common sight to see bodies strewn all over the plum-colored carpeting, on the stage, at the altar area, in the aisles. People throughout the sanctuary would moan and weep as they lay trembling.

Nightly, buses and vans from as far away as Minnesota and Quebec would pull up to the front of the church to drop off their load of passengers. Other visitors came from overseas as well—believers from Australia, Korea, Brazil, Uganda, Great Britain, continental Europe, people desperate to experience a touch from God.

Services began to attract five thousand people each night, double the number the sanctuary could hold. Work crews quickly installed closed-circuit television monitors in the chapel, the cafeteria, and the choir room to provide space for those who arrived too late to find a seat in the main sanctuary. A fourth room eventually had to be prepared for the overflow crowds. If you weren't at the church by mid-afternoon, you had very little chance of watching the service live that night.

The sanctuary was bursting at the seams. It wasn't even four years old, and already it was too small.

Kilpatrick and Hill began a routine of working fourteen- to sixteen-hour days. Ushers, altar workers, and maintenance workers had to be enlisted in record time. Security guards patrolled areas where worshipers parked their cars, often a half-mile or more from the church. Some services lasted until sunrise.

"I've never seen anything of this magnitude in a church anywhere," Elmer Melton told *Charisma* shortly after the revival broke out. At the time, he was responsible for opening and closing the church—a big job when the church is open nearly all the time.

"We've asked the Lord to break the bonds of darkness in the north, east, south, and west to let people in, and He's done it," he claimed.

The heightened activity at the church drew the attention of the media as well. The *Pensacola News-Journal,* the *Mobile* (Alabama)

Register, and a host of smaller publications sent reporters and photographers to cover the phenomenon. Local television stations joined in, and one night a producer from Donahue showed up, though the talk show went off the air before a segment on Brownsville was aired.

On another night the church allowed a photographer from a secular newspaper to set up his camera in the main aisle, something out of the ordinary since cameras and photographers can often be distracting. The photographer agreed to cooperate with the church's conditions; he intended to prevent his presence from intruding on whatever God might do.

"During an intense move of the Spirit, he fell on his knees, dropped his camera and began repenting," said Hill. "It's hard to hold a camera when people are screaming out for mercy. People who come to report on the revival have been blown away."

On another occasion, a man attended a service at Brownsville just hours after his girlfriend had been murdered. He'd had every intention of killing the person he thought was responsible—but before he could, a young person from the revival persuaded him to go to church instead. That night, he gave his life to the Lord.

The revival couldn't help but draw the attention of law enforcement officials as well. At first traffic jams around the church created something of a nightmare, until an orderly plan for getting cars in and out of the area could be developed. Reports of "drunken" drivers increased. It took some getting used to, but in time officers learned to distinguish people who were overcome by God from those who were overcome by alcohol.

Bill Langlitz, a regular at the services during the early days of the revival, readily saw the significance of what God was doing in their midst.

"God is pouring out His Spirit upon all flesh, as it says in [the Book of] Joel in the Old Testament," he told *Charisma*. "It started slowly, and then the Holy Spirit started flowing and coming upon the people. By word of mouth, the word spread about the manifestations of the Holy Spirit."

Once-reserved women—young and old— danced before the Lord in the aisles of the church, for the most part completely oblivious to the thousands of people in the pews, on the floor, and sharing the aisles with them. Caught in a moment of total abandonment in worship, the women expressed such freedom in their devotion to God that their joy was contagious. Soon enough, young men began to shed their inhibitions as they "danced like David."

Deftly avoiding the dancers, one family walked the church's aisles for hours during dozens of revival services. Carol DeLugo's special-needs child, Rachel, was at the time a four-year-old who needed to get up and walk around.

"Rachel has been really blessed by the revival," Carol told *Charisma* in the summer of 1995. "She definitely knows she's in the house of the Lord when she's here."

Rachel was far from the only child to be touched; children began to routinely lay hands on each other—and on adults—to pray for them.

And in the midst of all this, people began wondering just what to call this obvious move of God. Early on, the tag Brownsville Revival took root; another name used in the beginning that never quite caught on was The Father's Day Outpouring, because of the date on which it erupted. It's still also known as the Pensacola Outpouring. ("Sounds like an American soft drink," quipped one British journalist.)

Whatever it's called, by the end of the first year the revival was going so strong that Brownsville had to eliminate services on Tuesday and Saturday nights just to give volunteers a much-needed rest. And the church had developed its own orderly way of doing things, which it still maintains.

Whenever possible the preaching is followed by teenager Charity James singing "Run to the Mercy Seat." Next comes a bathroom break—an unusual but necessary addition to the schedule—followed by two or three specific altar calls. A prayer table is set up where people can put photos of their unsaved loved ones, books about issues they're having a problem with, articles of clothing, résumés, church bulletins—anything that symbolizes something someone wants prayer about.

And each night, ten rows in the sanctuary are reserved for visiting clergy. For those pastors who come seeking revival in their own churches, John Kilpatrick has a special message: "Revival is work—*major* work."

"Whenever a church or a pastor says, 'Let's make a little room for revival,' they're going to have to amend their whole lifestyle to accommodate a move of God," said Kilpatrick.

So will the members of the church. Some people left Brownsville even before revival broke out; they objected to Kilpatrick preaching about it so much. In all, thirty people left.

"Any pastor with a pastor's heart is going to grieve over people who leave—even people who caused you problems," he said, adding that about three hundred people have joined Brownsville since June of 1995. "But just as there are pastors who are not really ready for revival, there are also church members who are not ready for revival.

"You have to let God be God. I'm just an undershepherd. He is the great Shepherd. It's His church. The Lord will do His work, so I just need to stand aside and trust that He knows what He is doing."

Sixteen months into the revival, Pensacola itself was still feeling the effects of the power of God. Hotels, motels, and restaurants routinely offered discounts to those attending the revival. Travel agent Linda Fussell found herself busier than ever, booking flights to Pensacola or reserving rooms for more than a thousand visitors each week through her company, Global Travel.

"Nothing has drawn as many people to Pensacola as this revival has," Linda Fussell told *Charisma* in the fall of 1996. "We are on the telephone from the first thing in the morning until we close every day. I've never been this busy in my fifteen years in business."

Two years into the outpouring, Fussell could tell the revival was showing no signs of slowing down simply by the constantly ringing phones in her office. In the spring of 1997, her agency added two more phone lines to handle all the calls—bringing the number of lines to a total of six.

People in the city still scratch their heads and wonder, *Why Pensacola?* But as for Kilpatrick, he has no doubt why God chose to visit Brownsville.

"The Holy Spirit poured out His blessings on our church not because the pastor was so spiritual," he said. "The Holy Spirit saw the faithfulness of our people—and their love for God."

As strangers from nearby slums and far-away places began to crowd them out of their own church, that faithfulness and love would be sorely tested.

4

HARD-CORE EVANGELIST

THE MAN WHO BROUGHT all those strangers to Brownsville was at one time the last person you'd expect to find in a church, much less to find *successful* in a church.

Today, Hill will openly tell you he was tormented by evil forces from his early childhood. Born in Ankara, Turkey, in 1954, Hill was already drinking and smoking by the time he was ten and mainlining drugs at the age of sixteen. At the time, Hill understood little about the spiritual forces at work in his life. He only knew the life he was living—the life of a drug addict and dealer who had been arrested thirteen times before a faithful minister dared to believe that the heart of such a hardened rebel could be softened by the gospel of Jesus Christ. That was in 1975, and for the next twenty years Hill would undergo the preparation he needed in order to be ready for one of the greatest outbreaks of revival in the latter half of the twentieth century.

Trained in "hard-core evangelism" by the likes of David Wilkerson, Nicky Cruz, and the late Leonard Ravenhill, Hill and other students at Wilkerson's Twin Oaks academy in Texas learned soul-winning—or else.

"If you didn't learn, they'd kick you out," Hill remembers. "They'd teach us about evangelism, put us in a van, drive us to a dope party in Dallas, dump us out, and say, 'Go into that dope party. We'll pick you up at four in the morning.'

"You knew very quickly whether you were called to evangelism."

Hill was called, and he knew it. After graduating from the two-year academy, he joined a church ministry and took a group of young people to Mexico. It was there that he realized without a doubt that God's specific call on his life was to the mission field.

Like so many other leaders in the current worldwide renewal, Hill's life and ministry were profoundly touched and shaped by one of the leaders of the Argentine revival—a move of God that started in the early eighties, surged in 1992, and is credited with more than two million salvations.

On his first trip to Argentina, Hill attended a soccer-field evangelistic rally conducted by Carlos Annacondia, a former businessman who alone has led two million people to Jesus Christ. Hill watched in awe as Annacondia stayed until two o'clock in the morning, personally laying hands on each person who went forward for salvation, for healing, for a release of God's power in his life. Among those he laid hands on was Hill—and the evangelistic anointing on his life became more real than ever.

"I had never seen anything like that night," Hill said. "I saw fifteen- to twenty-thousand people craving God, going after God. Carlos was so common, so loving; all he cares about is that one little boy, that one grandpa, that one uncle that's coming to Jesus."

For seven years, Stephen Hill lived and worked in that spiritually charged atmosphere, and it was during that time that his passion for the lost was forever cemented in his ministry. He planted seven churches in South America and Eastern Europe, and helped build an orphanage that houses one hundred twenty-five children in Argentina.

As an Assemblies of God evangelist, Steve Hill was intrigued by reports of unusual Pentecostal practices being experienced at an Anglican church in London that had placed a high priority on evangelism. In January 1995, months before revival broke out in Pensacola, Hill traveled to London with every intention of meeting with Sandy Millar, vicar of Holy Trinity Brompton Church, to find out just what was going on at his church. After making an appointment with Millar, Hill went to the church for a service.

"I stepped over several bodies on my way in," recalled Hill, who estimated there were more than five hundred people on the floor, moaning and groaning. "To see English folks doing that was odd."

Soon Hill would join those bodies on the

floor. When Millar prayed for him, Hill fell out in the Spirit, experiencing a refreshing in his own spirit. Coming so close on the heels of a time when Hill was heavily involved with church planting overseas, this refreshing was sorely needed.

"It was as if the Lord put His arms around me and told me He loved me and would never leave me," Hill recalled. "It was a tender time with Jesus."

And in one sense, that's all it was. Hill sees little or no connection between his experience at Holy Trinity Brompton and the revival that would break out in Pensacola six months later—especially since nearly twenty leaders in addition to Sandy Millar had laid hands on him at different times.

"We confuse people when we say they have to go to this place or to that place to receive an anointing," he cautioned. "There's a whole lot more to it than that."

There certainly was a whole lot more to revival than Hill ever anticipated. After returning from England, Hill's agenda was full; it would have been tough to add anything else to his schedule for the rest of the year. But revival quickly taught him just how accommodating you can be when it's God who interrupts your agenda.

In the summer of 1995, Hill planned to travel to Russia, where he was to help build a church. But when revival broke out in Brownsville, Hill's plans changed abruptly, and he made a commitment to stay in Pensacola for as long as the revival lasted. Not only did he cancel his trip to Russia but the revival went on so long that he also relocated from his home in Lindale, Texas, to a rented house in Pensacola, bringing his wife and children along. Two years later, the revival was still in full swing, and the evangelist who said he would stay for the duration had bought a house in a nearby town in Alabama eighteen miles from the church. He settled in.

Hill describes the revival as a "divine interruption" in his life. "A divine interruption is when you're headed one way, and God wants to go in another way. This whole revival is a divine interruption. We all believe this will go on for several years." He made that statement in March 1996, and his own craving for Jesus, and the revival itself, is still as strong as ever.

"This is the opportunity of a lifetime," Hill told *Charisma*. "And the opportunity of a lifetime must be seized during the lifetime of the opportunity.

"It would be ludicrous for us to close up shop and say, 'Let's go golfing.' In America there is a famine for truth. As long as the people come, I will be here."

Like many other renewal leaders, Hill spends little time attempting to explain the manifestations. To Hill, the manifestations have both biblical precedence (in Acts, chapter 9, Paul was thrown to the ground by the power of God) and a wealth of historical precedence, including nineteenth-century revivalist Charles Finney's description of feeling "waves of liquid love" and being jolted on the floor. In Hill's own experience, he has discovered that while some people are able to simply make a decision for Christ, others need a more dramatic encounter.

"Many who have been shaken said that God was literally shaking them," said Hill. "I look for what God is doing in their lives.

"What I see in revival is brokenness, moaning, and groaning," Hill told *Charisma*. "At Brownsville, this isn't the laughing revival. This is more of an old-fashioned Southern revival meeting. The conversions and the baptisms have been our lifesavers.

"This is not meek and mild," Hill said of the revival. "This is the real McCoy."

For Hill, part of the evidence that validates the revival is the lack of focus on the leaders involved. The renewal worldwide—whether in the hot spots of Toronto or London or Pensacola or Pasadena—has been characterized as the "nameless, faceless revival" because of the absence of a star evangelist or central figure.

"Nobody is shining here," said Hill about Brownsville. "I will not take a drop of God's glory. It's all for Him."

Late in the summer of 1995, God's glory was about to break forth in another completely unexpected way, through the life of a teenaged girl.

5

THE
VIDEOTAPE

TWO MONTHS AFTER the revival broke out, a young college student stepped up to the pulpit at Brownsville Assembly. And while the regulars at the nightly services by now had come to expect the unexpected, God was about to throw them for another loop.

Alison Ward, then nineteen, was well-known to the local people in attendance that night. A member of the Brownsville church since she was five years old, Alison was a "second-generation" Christian who had been caught between her knowledge of God's Word and the ever-increasing lure of the world. She had just completed her first year of junior college when God unexpectedly showed up at her church.

To please her mother, Alison attended the nightly services for the first week. One night, Hill preached about the futility of trying to serve two masters. The Holy Spirit had nailed Alison Ward, and she knew it. Mustering up all the resistance she could summon, Alison refused to give in. But within just a few days, Alison couldn't take any more. She surrendered. The kingdom of God could claim another victory.

She spent two hours on the church floor that night.

Later that summer, the time had come for Alison to share her testimony publicly. The date was August 18, and as usual, thousands of people had come to the Friday night service—always a special time, since that was the one night of the week set aside to baptize new believers.

Introduced by Kilpatrick—who vouched for Alison's credibility—this obviously articulate young woman began to tell the crowd how God had convicted her of the spiritual compromise in her life. God's conviction had been so powerful, she said, that she had made a conscious, irreversible decision that she would no longer be a lukewarm Christian. She was sold out to Jesus.

But as Alison continued to speak, her head began to shake back and forth in such an unusual way that she appeared to be suddenly stricken with a severe neurological disorder. By the time she finished, a mere eight minutes later, the sanctuary was filled with the sound of deep groanings for the lost; the altar was filled with sinners seeking salvation. Pastor Kilpatrick buckled under the power of God and had to be carried to a chair, where he stayed for three hours, completely drunk in the Spirit.

Steve Hill would have no need to preach on this night. Alison Ward's testimony had provided all the altar call this church needed.

Hill and all the other church leaders in attendance that night were among those hit by the power of God. In all, two hundred people found salvation in that one service alone.

But the impact of Alison's testimony didn't

end there. Videotapes of her testimony began circulating and became such a hot item that the church could hardly keep up with the demand for more copies. The church sold thousands of copies of the video, and countless others have been duplicated and sent around the world. Churches continue to report that the power of God falls on their congregation at precisely the moment on the tape when Alison falls under the power of the Holy Spirit.

For a while, one pastor in Texas was so overcome by the spiritual force of Alison's testimony that he watched the video every day. A pastor in Jacksonville, Florida, collapsed in the pulpit under the power of God as the video was being shown during a service; people rushed to the altar in response.

A Baptist pastor admitted that at first he did not believe God would make anyone shake the way Alison did. He's since been converted: "God can do whatever He wants to do," he now says. "I don't care anymore [about my former theology]. I'm here to let God be God."

Alison herself had to learn to let God be God.

"I would shake. It was crazy," Alison told *Charisma*. "It looked terrible. But when it happened I would feel closer to God. I could feel the pain that the Holy Spirit feels for people. The Holy Spirit was bigger on the inside than my body could contain."

By the fall of 1996, Alison Ward had become something of a regular on the youth-group speaking circuit. When Alison speaks to kids, she pulls no punches. She lets them have it. After all, at one time she was a good church kid herself, and she knows full well how easy it is to talk the talk and fake the walk.

At the Thanksgiving weekend *Charisma* Family Conference in 1996, Alison briefly told the several hundred kids in attendance the story of her pre-revival life, and it was evidently one they could relate to. You could see it in their faces, in their eyes, in their silence. She was preaching to church kids, many of whom know what it's like to be forced to go to church and youth group—and to conferences.

Like the old Alison, so many of the teens in the room want to have their fun on Saturday night and sleep in on Sunday morning. But they go to church only to get their parents off their backs. They go to youth group only to keep up the appearance of being remotely interested in anything spiritual.

"I'd go to youth group, and they'd give altar calls," Alison continued. "I used to feel so sorry for the person giving the altar call. What if nobody got up?

"I had it all wrong. I should have been feeling sorry for myself. There I was sitting in my seat, and I was going to hell."

Alison, the good church kid, was also suicidal. "But I didn't have the guts to kill myself. I didn't have the guts to stand up for God or to stand up for sin," she said, her voice quivering with the obvious revulsion she feels each time she recounts the way she was before that June night at the Brownsville altar.

"We've gotten so religious, and we've gotten so bound up in who man says God is, that He's been pushed right out the door. We've forgotten about Him," Alison said. "We cannot sit around and be stale and dead and dry and never see the power and the move of God anymore and hope to live through these end days, hope to make it to heaven, hope to live for God on our own. It will not work. God is not playing around."

No matter where she is, as Alison speaks before a group of people her head shakes back and forth, seemingly uncontrollably. Sometimes it's difficult to watch, especially when it looks as if she's having trouble synchronizing the microphone and her constantly moving head. But she never misses a beat; it's clear that something supernatural is happening in her body, in her mind, and in her spirit.

For a long time, Alison wasn't exactly thrilled with the shaking. Back home in Brownsville, it was acceptable. Everyone was used to the manifestations, and hers fit right in. But out on the road, at unfamiliar churches, looking at the sea of unfamiliar faces, Alison didn't like the idea that she was becoming something of a weird spectacle spawned by the revival.

She asked God why He kept causing her to shake each time she publicly gave her testimony. In His very specific answer to her, He compared His Holy Spirit to the wind.

"You can't see the wind; you just see the effects of the wind," she said. "Whenever it's calm and still, you don't think about the wind.

That's how we have treated the Holy Spirit in our churches, in our youth groups, and in our lives. He's been like a gentle breeze—not strong enough for us to even hear Him or feel Him or know Him, because we wouldn't let Him in, we wouldn't let Him near."

By causing her to shake, Alison said, God is showing the kids the visible effects of the Holy Spirit. He's revealing Himself to the lukewarm, the young people who need a wake-up call, kids who are living half in and half out of the kingdom of God.

"You may think I'm putting this on or that I'm sick or I'm crazy. I'm none of those things," she said. "But when I stand before people, He shows Himself. It's time that God represents Himself, and He's here to do that."

She ended with a warning: "I'd advise you not to criticize, because you're criticizing the Holy Spirit."

It's tough to stay in your seat when Alison gives an altar call. The folks at Brownsville learned that in the summer of 1995, and youth throughout the Southeast are finding that out as well.

6
RADICAL
TEENS

THANKS TO ALISON WARD and a host of teens from Brownsville, it's pretty hip to know Jesus these days. But knowing Jesus means being far more than hip, and these kids have changed His name from being a curse word to being a blessing. They've started a youth revival that demands an all-out commitment to the Lord.

In the first eighteen months of the revival, the Brownsville youth group had grown from one hundred to four hundred active members, often with as many as seven hundred kids attending the meetings. Attending lively meetings with other Christian teens is by all means not the only "religious" thing they do: These kids leave the safe haven of the Brownsville church to go out as evangelistic teams, conducting assemblies in schools and ministering to inmates in area jails and prisons each week.

In 1995 only three campus ministries existed at Pensacola high schools and middle schools; now more than thirty are at work in the public schools. At one area high school, the revival conversion of the football team's quarterback prompted a mini-revival of its own among the students there.

The assistant principal of a local high school brings busloads of teenagers to Brownsville every Friday and Saturday night. His school of twenty-three hundred students had six known, professing Christians at the beginning of the 1996–1997 school year; by the spring of 1997 there were six hundred.

The revival's youth are known to wear Christian T-shirts and Brownsville arm-bands proudly, and openly carry their Bibles to school—something that would have been unheard of a few short years ago. Some even shake under the anointing of the Holy Spirit while they're in school; nurses and other school personnel are learning to take that in stride.

And youth groups at area churches are seeing unprecedented revival among their own ranks. The Pine Forest United Methodist Church youth group is one that has been touched by God in a powerful way through the Brownsville Revival. On Father's Day 1995, the Pine Forest youth group happened to be on a retreat—and youth director Linda Smith just "happened" to hold a special session devoted to the promised revival. They returned to Pensacola to find that revival was no longer just a promise. Full-blown revival had arrived.

Linda checked out Brownsville for herself, encouraged her youth group to attend, and urged them to take their parents along as well. She was sold on its validity.

One girl from Pine Forest had been dating a drug dealer. God touched her life through Brownsville, changed her direction, and so transformed her that she later assumed a leadership role. And now when the youth group meets for prayer for revival, they go one step further—they anoint the church pews with oil in anticipation of those who will come to be saved.

The Pine Forest Bible College has also attracted young people from other churches, including some from Brownsville Assembly of God. And among those is Alison Ward, who begins to shake whenever Linda Smith teaches on the Holy Spirit.

Smith believes today's youth are already in a fast-forward growth mode in terms of revival—unlike her own background. "I call myself a 'crockpot for Jesus' because I've been in preparation for so long," Smith said. "I believe the Jesus movement [in the early seventies] and the Charismatic movement were just preparation for today's move of God."

While the manifestations associated with Brownsville don't occur as frequently among adults at Pine Forest, they have affected the youth. The youth from the church became so drunk in the Spirit once, they had to be carried one at a time and placed into the church van to be taken home. They were "pulsating with the power of God," Smith said.

One family in particular, though, faced a prolonged time of upheaval until the parents recognized the work of the Spirit in their daughter's life. Their daughter had begun screaming as she experienced a vision of Jesus collecting all her sins, placing them in a bag, and discarding them.

"She couldn't talk normally for a week," Smith said. "She began to shake every time she got near the church."

The girl's mother "cried for a week," even missing work because she was so concerned about what was happening to her daughter. She thought her daughter had been ruined for life.

"Then the mother received the manifestation of shaking," Smith said. "Now she and her two daughters pray and shake constantly. This woman used to be full of worry and fear. She is changed forever."

Another woman who cried for days over what was happening to her daughters was the mother of Alison Ward. But her tears were tears of joy because she understood full well what God was doing.

"She knew God was also dealing with me," said Alison's younger sister Elizabeth, who was eighteen when the power of God took over her life.

Reared in the Brownsville church, Elizabeth rebelled and was looking forward to a time when she could move away from home and stop being forced to go to church. Her life had fallen into a routine of drinking hard liquor and taking cold medications so she could fall asleep. She had become so adept at lying and sneaking around that her parents were unaware she was drinking.

Every now and then she would ask God to change her life, but she felt as if she were talking to herself. Prayer just didn't work for her any longer.

"I didn't see anything real about altar calls," Elizabeth told *Charisma*. "I thought they were so fake that the people who went up just needed attention. I wasn't convicted of sin anymore."

Then revival hit.

For whatever reason, Elizabeth went forward one night for prayer. "I began shaking. It was like God was breaking all that hardness that was in me. God said He was cleaning me out. I was so stubborn. I didn't want to change."

For an hour and a half, Elizabeth laid on the floor, unable to open her eyes. When she got up, she wasn't quite sure what had happened because she didn't feel any different. But God had gotten through, and His pull on her life proved to be real.

The next time God's Spirit impacted her life, she knew she was changed.

"I felt as if God had taken hold of my hand, and He started moving it back and forth. God said, 'If you'll hold on to Me, you'll be all right. You can't turn back.'" That night, Elizabeth had to be carried home.

"I shook for three days. I was the last person you would have expected to shake on the floor of a church. People knew this was real when they saw it happen to me."

One of Elizabeth's newfound friends at Brownsville is Joseph Justiss. Something of a loner in his early years, Joseph was raised in an Assemblies of God church but felt that he never quite fit in. While working as a waiter in Orange Beach, Alabama, Joseph, then nineteen, got drunk one night, had sex with another man, and eventually became involved in the gay lifestyle. He later moved to Orlando, Florida, where he became immersed in homosexual promiscuity with partners he met in the city's many gay bars.

His lifestyle led him into the New Age movement, witchcraft, and clinical depression. After attempting suicide, Joseph was admitted to a hospital psychiatric unit. He moved to Pensacola following his release, and it was there that a witch told him that an Egyptian demon had entered his spirit. He returned to the gay lifestyle, and proclaimed his identity by having a nipple pierced and a gay tattoo branded onto his body.

Then his mother started attending Brownsville Revival meetings. Joseph agreed to attend one Sunday night.

"I was freaked out by the people," he told *Charisma.* "I was feeling so oppressed. I hated Steve [Hill]."

When he went home that night, though, he felt lonelier than ever. He decided to go back to Brownsville—not to attend another service but to kill himself in front of the church.

Instead, he went inside. During the altar call he began manifesting demons, and Steve Hill made a beeline for him. Joseph tried to run out the door, with Steve in hot pursuit.

Shivering, crying, and screaming, "Let me alone! Let me go!" Joseph began to break. As Steve cast one demon after another out of him, Joseph fell on the floor and began wrestling with Steve—who continued praying over him until there was no fight left in Joseph.

The following night, Joseph returned to Brownsville, stood up to go to the altar and fell forward on his face. There, on the floor, he gave his life to the Lord.

Joseph went home and immediately began filling garbage bags with those things that represented the garbage in his life—pornographic magazines and videos, witchcraft paraphernalia, crystals—took it all out to his backyard, doused the pile with kerosene, and put a match to it.

Today, Joseph works for a Christian television station and attends Bible college—a far cry from the lifestyle he used to lead.

Many of the young people who come to Brownsville found their way to the church through the adjacent rundown, drug-infested streets. Among those is Vikki Krasnosky, who lives in a depressed neighborhood near the church. Even though she herself wasn't saved, she began attending revival meetings and telling her gang-member friends that they would go to hell if they didn't get saved.

Her eighteen-year-old cousin, Jason, started attending the meetings. His brother Kevin, then age fifteen, who was also hanging out with the wrong crowd also came.

"There were a lot of drug houses in our neighborhood," Vikki told *Charisma*. "One drug dealer who was in Jason's band thought he was a wolf. He eventually overdosed, set himself on fire, and died."

Jason and the other band members got scared and started attending the revival. Now Jason is known as "The Fanatic" because of his faith in God. "All my friends started thinking I was a nut," said Jason. But peer pressure could not compete with the transforming power of God in Jason's life.

Vikki and other young people associated with the revival were living lives that were obviously changed. Yet they faced criticism from skeptics who continued to try to explain away what was going on.

"People in Pensacola had all kinds of funny explanations for what was happening at the church," Vikki said. "Some said there was ether on the people's hands [when they prayed over you], and that's what made you fall over. Others said there was something in the ventilation system."

You couldn't prove that by Tim Hanna, whose changed life extends far beyond the reaches of Brownsville's ductwork. The product of a not-so-perfect home life, Tim was planning to move to Atlanta for a more exciting future than he thought Pensacola could offer. But before he left, Vikki invited him to attend revival services at Brownsville Assembly—the first time he had ever attended church in his life.

Convicted of his sin—Tim was taking drugs and had gotten involved in witchcraft, among other things—he went to the altar full of hatred for his father. There, he found the answer to the gnawing emptiness in his life. He trembled as he felt God's presence for the first time ever.

"I found out that God will make you deal with things," Tim said. So he did. Now he spends his time reading the Bible, the one given to him by the Brownsville youth pastor, and the first one he has ever owned. And he has brought others to that same altar with him, including one friend who had been doing drugs with his own stepfather and another who describes the emotional rush of salvation as "better than drugs."

Parents, it seems, have a tough time accepting the revival, despite the changes in their children's lives. One teenager admitted to *Charisma* that his parents think all the kids touched by God at Brownsville are "fanatics"—definitely a derogatory term in their dictionary.

But that doesn't stop the young people from spreading the word about Jesus. They've become so fervent in their evangelism that at Brownsville Assembly they've come to be called the "Chain of Grace." As each new convert brings another friend or relative to the meetings, a chain reaction of conversions results. New believers are honored each night and are invited to sit in a reserved area on the front pew.

At times, the kids have no idea what's happening to them. Without any foundation in the church—or perhaps even *with* one—they have no frame of reference for their Brownsville experiences. One teenager named James broke into tears one night after he went forward for prayer. "I don't know what's happening," he said, "but it's wonderful!"

"So many of today's young people come from such dysfunctional homes," Kilpatrick told *Charisma*. "They've grown up never knowing love, intimacy, and closeness. When they come into this revival and feel the glory of God, it gives them such a warmth and feeling of intimacy. These kids just soak it in. They come by the hundreds.

"We've had kids here who have been molested, neglected, or unloved. The power of God comes on them, and it shakes them mightily. It's almost as if God is shaking something out of them. They leave looking so reconciled and peaceful."

"I love on the teens and pray for them," added Steve Hill. "Sometimes I pray for them all night long. They then bring in their unsaved friends. That's been the key to this revival: people bringing their unsaved friends and family.

"One Friday night a girl brought along fifteen unsaved friends. They do that all the time. Why? Because they know we're going to love them and pay attention to them.

"This is what I say to youth pastors:

When revival hits your church, love on these kids, then send them out as missionaries. They're new in the Lord and will make mistakes and do stupid things. But that's okay—I'd rather deal with that than with stale religion."

And stale religion can't cut it in this revival, as a full slate of denominational pastors would quickly find out.

7

A REVIVAL OF RECONCILIATION

T ONE POINT in late 1995, Steve Hill was getting so much mail that he had accumulated boxes of letters from pastors that he hadn't had time to open. Those he did open reflected such a cross section of denominations and streams within the body of Christ that a die-hard ecumenist would have swooned with envy.

"This revival is spreading all over the nation," said Hill. "I am inundated with letters from pastors who say they came to Brownsville, went back home, and then revival broke out in their church.

"It's flooding Iowa, mostly in the Assemblies of God churches. In Pensacola, we are seeing Methodists, Southern Baptists, and Episcopalians; a Catholic priest from Mobile just loves what's going on here. Mormons and Jehovah's Witnesses have been saved."

Add to that the countless nondenominational believers, Jews and Greek Orthodox who have crossed the threshold into the church since June 1995.

And while Hill's own denomination now officially endorses the Brownsville Revival, the leadership of the 2.5 million-member Assemblies of God (AG) adopted a cautious, "wait-and-see" attitude at first. Gradually, as more and more respected pastors and leaders within the denomination were singed by the revival fires, the Springfield, Missouri-based denomination began to embrace it. In early 1996 the revival literally moved in next door when a contingent from Brownsville— including Alison Ward—participated in services at Springfield's Central Assembly of God, adjacent to the AG headquarters.

"The AG is moving in this now," said

Hill. "We were born in the fire; we were the holy rollers. But we've become like all other denominations—institutionalized, sophisticated, educated. We have our temples on the corner of the interstate.

"We've lost the power, but we're coming back. Our leaders are saying, 'We'd better repent.'"

David Stevens, a conservative and respected presbyter with the Assemblies of God in Arizona, describes himself as the "chief of critics" of Brownsville and similar revivals. Stevens, pastor of the eight hundred fifty-member East Side Assembly of God in Tucson, wrote a letter to Assemblies of God general superintendent Thomas Task urging him to keep evangelist Benny Hinn—who has publicly embraced the renewal—out of the denomination.

"I resisted all of the falling," Stevens now says. "I like everything to be decent."

But he knew Stephen Hill personally, and so he traveled to Brownsville in October 1995. Someone there prayed for him.

"The next thing I knew I was on the floor, looking at the ceiling," Stevens recalls. "Something happened to me. I was shaking.

I had a spirit of intercession. There was such a desire for holiness."

So strong was that desire, in fact, that Stevens immediately called his wife and told her to cancel their subscription to HBO. And once he returned home, it was clear that he had brought the revival with him—as he discovered the following Sunday morning.

"After I had preached for only fifteen minutes, hundreds of people came running to the altar," said Stevens. "We didn't get out of there until three P.M."

With drug addicts coming to the church and finding deliverance and salvation, Stevens finds little reason to debate the validity of the renewal. He is a changed man ("God had to knock the pride out of me," he said), as are the unbelievers who have fallen under the conviction of God at the services he's conducted since returning from Brownsville. Still, he faces rejection within his own denomination.

"Many of my AG colleagues are skeptical," Stevens told *Charisma*. "A lot of my friends aren't calling me anymore. I know why they're cautious—they've seen a lot of frivolous things in the past."

To Stevens, the Pensacola Outpouring is anything but frivolous. And he has no doubt that in time, the individual Assemblies of God churches will come around.

Saying "amen" to that is Dan Livingston, pastor of the First Assembly of God in Pensacola—and an admitted former critic of the Brownsville Revival.

"This revival would not have started in my church," Livingston told *Charisma*. "I was too critical. This revival came to Pensacola in spite of us, not because of us."

In spite of himself, Livingston visited Brownsville out of curiosity. After stepping over bodies just to get into the church, Livingston made that decision typical of so many who now embrace the renewal. "I said, 'I am not going to fall on the floor.' Three and a half hours later, I got up. The river of God's Spirit has been flowing in my church ever since."

Livingston's six hundred fifty-member church witnessed two hundred conversions in the first year of the renewal. His church now includes former strippers, drug addicts, alcoholics, and gang members, in addition to AIDS victims and wealthy couples with condos on the Gulf Coast.

The river of revival started to flow in Livingston's church shortly after God gave him a telling insight into his own theology. "God said to me, 'My river is not going to fit into your box.' To be in the middle of the river you have to let go of control," he said. Today, Livingston sees his share of desperate pastors who say they have been in a dried-up riverbed.

Since revival broke out, Livingston has taken this move of God beyond his own congregation. He took it out of town, out of state, out of denomination—to New Life Baptist Church in Wynne, Arkansas, about forty-five miles west of Memphis.

"The power of God fell all over this Baptist church," said Livingston, who credits the validity of the Brownsville Revival with its emphasis on salvation. "Every true out-pouring has one focus: to reach the lost."

Because the crowd at Brownsville is so diverse, counselors ask those who go forward for salvation or repentance what their denominational backgrounds are. People are referred to area churches when possible, but many of the visitors to the church are not only from out of town but also from out of state. The church staff keeps tabs on other churches throughout the country that are either already flowing in renewal or have at least experienced stirrings of revival.

Among those churches is one that belongs to a denomination not generally connected with things charismatic—Pine Forest United Methodist Church, where the youth have experienced such a powerful encounter with God. Perry Dalton has served as pastor of the Pensacola church for seven years.

"There's always been a charismatic undercurrent," Dalton said about his church. "We've been experiencing gradual renewal for several years.

"We've been praying for revival for years, although we didn't know it would come in this form. Worship over the years has become more contemporary, instead of just singing Hymn 96 and sitting down."

The church's fourteen prayer groups meet on a regular basis, with an emphasis on revival. A Saturday night prayer and praise service generally lasts about an hour, but the Sunday night service is "open-door" night. ("We just open the door and let whatever happens happen," Dalton explains.)

"We are basically returning to our roots," said Dalton. "We are becoming the enthusiasts that John Wesley talked about. Our people are on fire. They are eager to share their faith. My role is to keep it from blowing up.

"Every now and then somebody's cage gets rattled, but we have not had a mass walkout. The older people aren't as rattled because they remember what it used to be like in the old days. But the middle-aged crowd is having a hard time with it."

Dalton's seven hundred-member church passed the century mark some time ago— but at one time, its future was threatened by the growing influence of the New Age movement and occultism, particularly by followers of psychic Edgar Cayce. What saved his church was the Charismatic movement. Dalton himself had been baptized in the Spirit in the seventies, and despite his denomination's coldness toward the renewal, he chose to remain a Methodist.

He first heard about the revival at Brownsville just after he returned from vacation in June 1995. He admits to being fearful at first, but the urgings of people he trusted prompted him to give the church a try.

"I realized that Steve Hill was not there to promote himself or to make everybody Assemblies of God," Dalton told *Charisma*. "I became very comfortable with it after I got used to stepping over bodies."

Dalton's understanding of revival—both in its historical and contemporary perspectives—has been deepened by the addition of program director and youth leader Linda Smith to the church's staff. A longtime student of revival, Smith was baptized in the Spirit in 1963 at Asbury College in Wilmore, Kentucky, and later joined the staff of Campus Crusade for Christ. While there, she led twelve staff members in the baptism in the Holy Spirit at a time when it was "illegal" to speak in tongues while employed by the organization.

Since coming to Pine Forest in 1989, Smith has been telling her youth group that God was going to use them for a great End-Time revival, and she started praying for revival every Sunday evening in the Upper Room service.

"I had never in my life seen the shaking,

even though I had read about it in history books," she told *Charisma.* "But we tend to forget that.

"I had never heard anybody yelling 'Fire! Fire! More! More!' It was like a cadence," she continues, describing her first encounter with the Brownsville Revival. "Dry wood makes a great fire," Smith said. "The revival fire now blazing is evidence that we were so dry."

While Methodists who would never have attended an Assemblies of God church have experienced the revival fire through Pine Forest, not all the news in the Methodist camp is good. Families have left Pine Forest out of the parents' fear that their children would be exposed to revival. One Methodist pastor was forced to resign his pastorate after he was baptized in the Spirit during a service at Brownsville.

Despite opposition, Linda Smith remains optimistic. Denominational leaders are clearly curious about what is going on at Pine Forest—especially in light of the church's continued growth. Nationwide, the nine million-member strong United Methodist denomination loses about a thousand members each week.

"We haven't lost one person to Brownsville Assembly," Smith told *Charisma.* "Our members don't miss our activities [in favor of Brownsville services]. Our people have taken leadership roles in this revival. Some of our people serve as prayer counselors at Brownsville and have reserved seating in the balcony."

Dalton himself has baptized people at Brownsville—"in the interest of being ecumenical."

"We are so hungry in the United Methodist Church for renewal that there is a desire for the Holy Spirit to work. It may take a decade, but eventually we will be open to whatever is necessary," Smith said. "I see revival coming to the United Methodist Church."

Another large group touched by the revival are Baptists, and among the churches most significantly touched is Second Baptist Church in Macon, Georgia, whose pastor, Gary Folds, got his first taste of renewal at Toronto Airport Christian Fellowship. He later traveled to Brownsville Assembly and now holds charismatic-style services at his church on Saturday nights. About five hundred people attend, and many end up on the floor, weeping and laughing.

Once a vocal critic of the Charismatic movement, Folds is now on the receiving end of the same criticism he used to dish out.

"This is not a label issue," said Folds, who said he has not forced charismatic practices on his church. "The issue is whether you are full of the power of God."

David White, former pastor of Calvary Baptist Church in Columbia, Mississippi, is also a Baptist, but don't tell him he can't be charismatic as well.

After being baptized in the Spirit in 1981, White chose to stay in the Southern Baptist Convention (SBC). "I knew God was going to bring revival to the SBC," White said with the confidence of one whose faith in God is unshakable.

After making two trips to Brownsville, White saw true revival hit his church in January 1996 when his congregation staged a production of the evangelistic drama *Heaven's Gates Hell's Flames*. The planned three-night run extended to three weeks; his one hundred forty-member church recorded twelve hundred decisions for Christ during that time.

"Columbia has never seen anything like this," White told *Charisma*. "The first person saved was a black teenager—in a heavily racist area. Older conservatives at Calvary were not happy about the crowds, the blacks coming, or the hand raising [during worship]."

But God had His way despite the opposition. People began to shake during services, and once, when a handkerchief was sent from Brownsville, White's wife fell out under the power of the Spirit as soon as the package containing the handkerchief was opened. A reporter sent by the Columbia paper to cover the unusual revival at the church—which was causing traffic jams in the town of seven thousand—was saved.

"[Our people] are ready to break out," White said. "Tradition has held them back, but they are ready to bust loose."

Fred Wolfe is another Southern Baptist who will have nothing to do with the widespread notion that Baptists are anti-charismatic. As pastor of the four thousand-member Cottage Hill Baptist Church in Mobile, Alabama, some seventy miles west of Pensacola, Wolfe makes regular trips to

Brownsville. At least ten of his church members serve as prayer counselors. For a while some of his deacons attended every service—the whole time "drunk in the Spirit and shaking on the front row."

He's even preached at Brownsville. In March 1996, Wolfe used the vision of Ezekiel to encourage the congregation to "jump into the river of God—not just ankle deep but over our heads." At his own church, he has been known to preach spirited sermons about "swimming in the river of God," a typical Brownsville theme.

He said he has no fear of retribution from others in the SBC over his involvement with Brownsville, even though a similar revival has broken out in his church.

"You make decisions along the way, and sometimes they are difficult," Wolfe told *Charisma.* "They may be perceived by people as bold steps, but I want more of God. I always want to be in a place where I can be led of God."

True to his Baptist leanings, Wolfe has also been careful to teach his congregation to test any and all manifestations for biblical authenticity.

"It would be idolatrous for anyone to seek a sign instead of [seeking] God. That is my message," said Wolfe, adding that he doesn't understand many of the things that seem to be going on in the spiritual realm. "You're to test any phenomenon by the Word of God. Does it give the individual a hunger for God? Does it lead them to a holy life? Does it make them love Jesus more? If it does these things, it is of God."

For now Wolfe has chosen to remain in the SBC, unlike former Baptist pastor Richard Daniels. As pastor of McCullough Baptist Church in rural Escambia County in the Florida panhandle, Daniels faced pressure to leave the SBC because of his Pentecostal leanings. To stop the "dissension and discord among the brethren" of the SBC, he left the denomination and formed an independent fellowship. Now called McCullough Christian Center, the congregation of the nondenominational church enjoys new freedom in worship.

"McCullough had always been Southern Baptist, but there was a Pentecostal flavor to our worship of God," said Daniels, who was baptized in the Holy Spirit while serving as chaplain of a nearby prison. "There was a desire among our people to see our church go forward. We didn't want to just be keepers of the aquarium; we wanted to move out and fish for men."

Many of the members of the church discovered the power of the Holy Spirit at Brownsville Assembly. "We were strengthened spiritually by what is taking place at Brownsville," Daniels told *Charisma*. "We've benefited from the revival because many of the people that we have in our church went to Brownsville and were filled.

"As a result many of them could not find places to worship behind that experience, because they were members of Baptist and Presbyterian churches and others. We have a mixture of all denominations in our church, so many of those who experienced Brownsville came to our church and found a spiritual haven."

Today, the man who once preached against the baptism in the Holy Spirit finds it difficult to comprehend the continued opposition to charismatic practices.

"I don't understand how any denomination can oppose the Pentecostal experience in this day and time, because people from all faiths are being filled," Daniels said. "God is destroying barriers, walls, and denominational lines. I believe the Southern Baptists are having to face that today. They don't want to, but they're being forced to."

For Kilpatrick, revival has changed the way he views the body of Christ. He illustrates his new perspective in this way:

> There's a story about an American flying across the Atlantic to England. It was planting season, and when he looked down and saw the stone fences and the geometric designs in the English countryside, he thought it was so beautiful.
>
> He stayed in England for several months. Then, when he flew back to America, back across the same area, the fences were all gone. He asked the flight attendant what happened to the fences. She said, "Oh sir, it's harvest time. The wheat is now higher than the fences, so you can't see them."

"What has blessed me about this revival is

that I no longer look at denominations," said Kilpatrick. "I can't see the fences. I look at the wheat—the harvest."

And the harvest, he said, is a good one, no matter what brand name others may try to place on it.

8
THE CANADIAN
CONNECTION

ON FEBRUARY 22, 1996, the revival service was proceeding as usual. As was his custom, John Kilpatrick asked the crowd of two thousand to raise their hands in response to a series of questions he typically asked: "Where are my Methodists?" "Any visitors from South America here tonight?"

One question brought an unusually warm reception from the crowd. "Who's here from Canada?" Everyone who's anyone in revival circles knows the impact Canada—

especially the Toronto Airport Christian Fellowship—has had on the worldwide renewal, and the people of Brownsville wanted this small contingent of Canadians to know how much they appreciated their faithfulness to God.

Little did they know that John Arnott, the man whose faithfulness to God sparked the renewal, was among the visitors that night.

John Arnott is a man who is hard to miss once you know him, easy to miss if you don't. Like so many other leaders in the current move of God, Arnott takes great pains to never attract attention to himself. He dresses casually, carries his own bags through hotels and airports and generally stays out of the limelight, which he somehow manages to do even when he's the main speaker. When John Arnott leads a service, Father God always takes center stage. His conversational preaching style—and the ease with which he steps over bodies without skipping a beat—stands in stark contrast to the flamboyancy and glitz of so many preachers during the height of the Charismatic movement.

Despite Arnott's unassuming, back-of-the-church presence that night, Kilpatrick spotted him and invited him to come forward to field questions from the congregation. In typical John Arnott fashion, he complied, though he had traveled to Brownsville simply to receive whatever God would offer him there.

A month earlier, Arnott had told *Charisma* that he was trying to free up a few days in his schedule so he could visit Pensacola.

"What they're doing at Brownsville is even greater than what's happening here [in Toronto]. That's true revival in Pensacola," he said. "We have salvations, but it's nothing like what's happening in Brownsville.

"We're stuck at the shallow end of the pool. Other places [like Brownsville] have gone deeper."

Later that year, another contingent from Toronto made an unassuming appearance at Brownsville. This group included Rick D'Orazio, an associate pastor of Queensway Cathedral. Queensway, the largest Pentecostal church in the greater Toronto area, is affiliated with the Pentecostal Assemblies, the Canadian branch of the Assemblies of God.

At Brownsville, D'Orazio came face-to-face with God—and with his own judgmental attitudes. A longtime critic of Toronto Airport Christian Fellowship (TACF), D'Orazio had never made the trip across town to see what was going on at TACF.

"When we started the church in Toronto, a few families from Queensway left and started coming to our church, so our relationship with Queensway was a little strained," Arnott told *Charisma*. "When revival broke out we called Rick and invited him to come and see what was going on, but he distanced himself from it."

To say that Rick "distanced" himself from Arnott's Toronto church is an understatement. Instead of traveling a couple of miles across the city to TACF, he traveled a thousand miles to the Florida panhandle to check out the revival. The revival there, after all, was endorsed by his own denomination, the Assemblies of God. That meant it either had to be authentic—or he had to see for himself how on earth his denomination could be taken in by such a thing.

His heart was beginning to soften, to entertain the idea that God might actually be at work in Pensacola. But before the worship began during his first service at

Brownsville, Rick suddenly thought of John Arnott and the renewal going on at TACF. He thought, too, of his own arrogance, judgmentalism, and jealousy that God had chosen to visit a church other than his. He knew what it was like to be a Michal, who despised David as he danced for joy before the Lord.

What God also revealed to D'Orazio at Pensacola was that *He* endorsed the Toronto Blessing as well as the Brownsville Revival and that *His* endorsement happened to be the one that mattered.

A repentant D'Orazio returned to his church in the Toronto suburb of Etobicoke, determined to call Arnott and ask his forgiveness. Knowing he would face opposition from both his own flesh and the devil, he drove to TACF to make an appointment with Arnott when he was unable to get through by phone. A month later, he sat in Arnott's office, openly confessing his pride, arrogance, and jealousy.

"I didn't even know he had ever said anything critical of us," said Arnott, adding that Rick's comments against TACF had been largely confined to his own congregation.

On Sunday, October 6, 1996—with Arnott's blessing—Rick took the pulpit at TACF, poured out the whole story of his opposition to the renewal and to TACF, and asked forgiveness from the members of the church as well.

They readily gave it. In fact, the people all stood up and cheered. One thing the revival sites have in common—whether in North America or Argentina or Europe or Korea—is a deep understanding of the power of forgiveness and the absolute necessity of extending forgiveness to others.

Sensing that this public act of forgiveness needed to go one step farther, Arnott asked everyone who had attended Queensway at any time in the past to stand. Among those standing—Arnott himself, who had been a part of the Queensway family years earlier. Forgiveness flowed from Queensway to TACF, from TACF to Queensway.

On the platform at a church in Canada, the reconciliation that had begun in Pensacola came full circle.

9

WHAT ABOUT THE
MANIFESTATIONS?

L EADERS OF THE CURRENT worldwide
renewal often face criticism from
people who believe they have invented
a new and manipulative way to bring people—
and their money—into the fold. But there's
almost nothing new about this revival. Only
the names, faces, and means of spreading the
revival have changed.

The Pensacola Outpouring in particular
resembles the Methodist camp meetings of
the early 1800s, most notably the Cane
Ridge Revival of 1801, say several historians.

That revival—which drew twenty thousand people to a small church west of Lexington, Kentucky—is credited with spawning the modern evangelical movement in the United States. And, much to the chagrin of many contemporary evangelicals, it was characterized by people shaking, jerking, shrieking, and swooning in ecstasy at services led by Methodist or Presbyterian preachers. People were thrown to the ground and slain in the Spirit. "Women would be jerking so violently that their hair would crack in the air like a driver's whip," said Steve Hill.

That kind of behavior often accompanied past revivals; people overwhelmed by a sense of God's holiness would fall to the floor. Nineteenth-century evangelist Charles Finney was among them. He described being jolted by "waves and waves of electricity" from heaven.

"United Methodism was founded with this kind of enthusiasm," Linda Smith, who has been studying revivals since 1968, points out. "The same thing you see in Brownsville is what you would have seen two hundred years ago. It's nothing new in Methodism."

The shaking and falling to the ground,

Smith adds, bothered the denomination's founder, John Wesley, "but it followed him wherever he went." People would fall prostrate, weeping and wailing. After one prayer meeting in 1739, Wesley wrote:

> At about three o'clock in the morning, as we were continuing in prayer, the power of God came mightily upon us. Many cried out in complete joy. Others were knocked to the ground. As soon as we recovered a little from that awe and amazement at God's presence, we broke out in praise.

The same behavior occurred in the late 1700s in services led by Francis Asbury, considered the father of American Methodism, and Peter Cartwright, a Methodist circuit rider in the early 1800s. Cartwright would not ordain any man who did not manifest outward displays of an inward conviction of sin. In his time, people would fall out of their pews during the sermon, overwhelmed with the conviction of their own sinfulness.

Cartwright unknowingly prophesied the future of the United Methodist Church in

America. He predicted: "If ever the Methodists get to the point that academics become more important than the power of the Spirit we will become as dead as any other denomination."

By the time the Azusa Street revival hit in 1906, the denomination had become so wealthy and powerful that the once revival-minded United Methodists flatly rejected the work of the Spirit in Los Angeles, Smith said.

What is happening at Pensacola, she added, is the kind of revival that happens only once or twice a century.

"A true revival, according to church history, is spontaneous and occurs sovereignly among church people much like spontaneous combustion, [which occurs when] the conditions are perfect to start a fire," said Smith, who has visited Brownsville several dozen times since the first week of the revival. "The right conditions for a spiritual fire among God's people are a widespread hunger for God and a yearning for righteousness due to wickedness and violence in the land."

And that's the essence of revival for Steve Hill as well—changed lives.

"It doesn't make any difference to me if you shake all night," said Hill. "If you're not changed the next day, then it's not worth anything. Any time you focus on the manifestations, you're majoring on the minors." The focus at Brownsville is always on repentance and salvation, and people whose manifestations distract from the message are escorted out of the sanctuary and into a private room.

Talk to any old-line Assemblies of God member, someone in their seventies or eighties, and chances are they once witnessed the kinds of manifestations of the Spirit that characterize the present revival. Why, then, are these manifestations so controversial?

It's obviously difficult to know how many people, if any, were faking the manifestations in the historical revivals. But there's no doubt that today, probably every revival leader has had to face that reality at some time. Hill and Kilpatrick have learned to develop an orderly way of handling people who get in the flesh during their meetings.

"Some people may be overzealous; sometimes their behavior reflects a need for love," said Hill, adding that Brownsville leaders attempt to be tolerant of people who may be disturbed. "We let them stay in this environment, where the glory of God is so thick that after a while they get their mind off themselves. They begin to get serious with God."

As in all things, the emphasis is on love —and prayer. "We pray God's blessing on them. We try to deal with it very delicately instead of reacting harshly."

10
OUT ON THE STREETS

IN 1995 BROWNSVILLE Assembly of God was something of an anomaly. Its upper-middle-class congregation attended services in a church building in a depressed area of town. Surrounded by bars, pawn shops, and used-car lots, the church used to be open for the most part only when services were being held. Not anymore.

In the two years since revival broke out, business people and community leaders have shared the pews with drunkards, drug addicts, prostitutes, and gang members.

"There's something that defies logic [here] because of the number of people getting saved off of drugs," Hill said. "We've always known this is a sin-infested area, with a lot of homosexuality, drug addiction, and witchcraft."

But Brownsville is one revival hot-spot that has broken down the walls separating the church and the community, much like the former Sunderland Christian Centre in Northeast England. In Sunderland, the impact of the renewal posed such a threat to the crime element in the city that ex-gang members who had found new life in Christ also found that their very lives were in danger.

While the situation in Pensacola is hardly as dramatic, the similarities between the two centers of revival do closely parallel each other. Both Sunderland on the North Sea and Pensacola on the Gulf of Mexico are port cities, with Sunderland being a center for commercial trade while Pensacola's naval air station draws military traffic. Both cities attract the prostitution trade as well, and those who profit off that trade don't like it when their girls and their pimps get saved, therefore stopping their cash flow.

In Pensacola, at least, the crime rate has dropped at times since the revival began, though law enforcement officials are reticent about attributing the drop to the revival. In 1996, the juvenile crime rate dropped 13 percent in Escambia County, while it rose 1 percent statewide. In the first six months following the revival, the overall crime rate fell 17 percent, the sheriff of Escambia County told Pastor Kilpatrick.

Pensacola's mayor, John R. Fogg, said he has not yet discovered a "downside" to the Brownsville Revival.

"I haven't heard a negative word about what is going on at the church," said Fogg, who has not attended services at the Brownsville church. "It's brought nothing but positive exposure to our community."

Positive exposure is something Fogg can appreciate more than most people. He had been in office just over seven hours when an anti-abortion activist gunned down an abortion doctor and his escort outside a clinic in Pensacola. That was July 29, 1994, and the media spotlight began to shine a decidedly negative light on the city. Less than a year later, the revival broke out.

"What I hear people in this city saying about Brownsville is 'Thanks,'" said Fogg.

Stephen Hill is far more bold in making the crime-drop/revival connection, crediting the reduction in crime to the number of prostitutes, drug addicts, and gang members who have been converted. One topless dancer with a six thousand-dollar-a-week drug habit was among those who made it to the altar one night to surrender her life to Jesus; she's one of many in that lifestyle who have found freedom at the Brownsville altar.

"A fear of God is developing in this city," said Hill. "The local people know that God is moving here. It gives [unbelievers] the creeps."

Still, the unbelievers come, leaving their guns and their drugs at the altar. Child molesters and pornographers openly confess their sin, repent, and find new life in Christ.

Hill cautions new believers against returning to their old friends and their old hang-outs, no matter how much they want to share their newfound faith with people whose lives are just as wasted as theirs used to be.

A topless dancer who worked at a local top-of-the-line club called Babes was among those whose enthusiasm for the things of God clouded her thinking: She wanted to return to the club where she once worked to witness to patrons and her former co-workers. Fortunately, she asked Steve Hill for his advice. His answer was a resounding no.

"She had been saved only about three days. That was definitely not the time for her to go back to the club," Hill said. "I told her, like I tell all new Christians, you need to grow in God. You can witness to your friends elsewhere—just don't go back into the bars."

Evidently, his advice was sound; people are coming to the church to get saved anyway. They're coming not just from the streets of Pensacola but from the streets of cities across the country. But they're bringing with them a host of problems, and sometimes, a host of demons, like a woman from Minneapolis who was saved at the Brownsville altar after immersing herself in witchcraft for the previous seven years. Situations like hers have given rise to a deliverance ministry.

Early on, Kilpatrick said, he recognized the demonic influence in the lives of so many hurting people who came to Brownsville for relief from torment. To help them, he created a team of prayer warriors trained especially for this vital ministry need. When they detect the presence of demonic influence in an individual, they're careful to remove the person from the sanctuary and do spiritual warfare in a separate room. That way, the congregation is protected from demonic activity, and the person is afforded a measure of privacy.

But many who come are those who have simply discovered that they have reached the end of themselves.

Like so many others at Brownsville Assembly, Teresa Finch began attending the services at the urging of her children. At thirty-seven, Teresa had not been to church for twenty years. A habitual pot user ("I wouldn't leave the house without a joint," she admitted) who was also addicted to soap operas and talk shows, Teresa had slipped into a severe depression by October 1995.

"I was ready to kill myself," she said. "My life was miserable; I had hit bottom."

But that month Teresa finally gave in and went to Brownsville, even though she believed the hypocrisy she had witnessed in the Pentecostal church she attended as a child had steeled her against ever having faith in Christians again. The first three times she attended Brownsville, she left before the altar call. The fourth time, she told God she would give Him a chance.

"I went down to the altar and told Steve [Hill] I was giving up drugs. I never touched them after that."

With Teresa Finch's salvation that night, the "chain of grace" went into effect within her social sphere. Within a few months, fifteen more people experienced God's grace as a direct result of her decision to give her life to Christ.

11

RESTORATION

ONE THING THIS revival has confirmed is that God is certainly no respecter of persons. He's not only drawing the street people, the aimless youth, the people whose lifestyles of bar-hopping and joint-smoking run counter to that of the typical churchgoer but He wants respectable people too, those who seemingly have it all together but whose lives are falling apart. Through Brownsville, He's attracting a true cross section of the American population that includes the wealthy, the successful, the rising stars.

Take JoAnn Lowell. For workaholics like her, going to church can cut some serious time out of the work week. But even workaholics can find themselves starving to death, and spiritually, that's just what was happening to JoAnn. She was starving.

While attending a Baptist church in Blairsville, Georgia, JoAnn heard about the Toronto-style worship at Brownsville—a seven-hour drive away—and immediately believed God was not only in it but He wanted her to be in it as well. In December 1995, she attended her first meeting there. JoAnn, a senior sales director with Mary Kay Cosmetics, was so hungry for the power of God in her life that she opted to go to the revival instead of to a Mary Kay convention.

"I went expectant, no matter what God wanted to do," she said. "You can feel the power of God when you walk in that place; the first night I went forward for prayer six times. I spent the whole night on the floor, although nothing else happened to me that I was aware of."

JoAnn bought a Brownsville worship tape, and each time she played the tape at home, she would fall on the floor and begin wailing and crying just from hearing the music.

"I didn't have a clue what was going on," she said. "I just knew it was the anointing of God."

In time, JoAnn did sense a significant change in her life. Her love for God became intense, overwhelming, indescribable. At times she felt as if she were in the holy of holies, completely aware of God's presence and omnipotence—as well as her own unworthiness. Her awareness of her need for repentance became more real than ever.

Meanwhile, the rest of her home life was not so glorious. Her husband, Robert, had been raised in the Baptist church but had been running from the Lord for thirty years, ever since he began to backslide as a teenager. Their marriage had been struggling, and it was going to take a miracle to save it. As a debt collector, Robert intimidated people for a living. He could drink straight vodka and still conduct business. His business style carried over into his home; he intimidated his wife and children, lost his temper, and verbally abused his family.

Like JoAnn, Robert loved his lucrative job—at the time, he was head of a statewide credit bureau in Georgia—and the material things it provided for him.

One of those things was a condo on the Gulf Coast. In mid-January 1996 Robert planned to look near Pensacola for a beach-side condo. On January 11, JoAnn had been at Brownsville for a service that came to be known as "Glory Night"—a true Jericho experience. "The praise and worship was like I had never experienced in my life," she said. "I broke loose and danced before the Lord."

To JoAnn's surprise, Robert agreed to watch the Alison Ward video—on their big-screen television, no less. "Holy rollin' stuff," he called it. The altar call gave him a cold chill.

When Charity James began to sing "Run to the Mercy Seat," Robert Lowell began to cry. "This scares me to death," he managed to say. He felt as if he had the dry heaves.

JoAnn touched him, and a sensation like an electrical shock charged through his body. His arm became so hot and the pain so intense that he yanked his arm away from JoAnn's reach.

"I scooted away from her," Robert recalls.

"All of a sudden, I ran to the phone, called a friend, and continued crying as I said, 'Something is going on. I just saw God on TV.'"

The next time JoAnn went to Brownsville, Robert just about scared the socks off some Georgia state troopers when he left home in a snowstorm, determined to make it to Pensacola with one purpose in mind—to get his wife and take her home.

"When I opened the door to the church, I felt as if I were going to pass out," Robert said. "I felt as if I were encountering some kind of radiation, something that was x-raying me."

Once he found JoAnn, the verbal abuse began despite the fact they were in church. Seated on the front row, he berated her with angry sarcasm, grilling her about such things as how much money she was giving to the church. Through an hour and a half of praise and worship, Robert lashed out at his wife.

"All I could think was, *If he can talk like this in church, what's it going to be like when we get home?*" JoAnn recalled. "I was sure there was going to be hell to pay. He looked like he was falling apart."

Meanwhile, a group of intercessors who couldn't help but notice his obnoxious scowl went to another room and began praying down the heavens on him. As the music continued, Robert began to feel like a marked man, but he didn't know why.

It was time for JoAnn to share her testimony. There, in front of hundreds of people and her own husband, she testified about her decision to follow Jesus. "I'm not going to listen to man anymore," she said.

That did it. According to Robert's way of thinking, his own wife had just told everyone there that she was not going to love him anymore. When it came time for prayer, Robert's mind was made up—he was not going forward, and he definitely was not going to end up on the floor the way his wife always seemed to.

That night, Pastor Kilpatrick changed his altar call just enough to force Robert's hand when he called for all the married couples to come forward. Reluctantly, Robert complied—though he steered JoAnn to one end of the altar and did his best to hide.

But his days of hiding from God were clearly numbered, and the number that came up was zero. Kilpatrick walked right up to Robert, looked him in the eye, and said, "The Lord has told me to tell you, son, that it's okay to receive the Lord. Relax and receive."

"He put his hand on my forehead, and I just blew up," Robert said. "I thought, *I don't even know you!* Then he prayed for me in tongues, and another young man prayed for me, and I just stared him down."

Robert bolted for the door, stepping over the ubiquitous Brownsville bodies along the way. Steve Hill ran after him and touched him—and that was it for Robert. He was knocked against a wall and slain in the Spirit.

"I was healed like that," he said, snapping his fingers. "I was healed of a football injury to my back. I was healed of cigarette addiction. I was healed of alcohol consumption. I became a man of honor and integrity."

After the service that night, at the same beach where he had begun to backslide thirty years earlier, Robert Lowell had all the "nastiness and venom and crud" squeezed out of him. "My mind was clean," he said. "My lungs felt clean. It was awesome; I cried for seven hours, all the way home to Blairsville."

The man that people had once been afraid of—by his own admission, nobody could work with him, and everyone cleared out when he entered the break room at work—was a changed man. Back at work, he established new policies—including one against sending threatening letters to debtors. Although it meant running the risk of losing clients, Robert injected a dose of kindness and mercy into his debt-collection business. Instead of failing, his business began to turn around.

"I had a house on the river, a car, a boat, a place here, a place there—and none of it mattered anymore," said Robert, who publicly asked the forgiveness of his church family—and was privately reconciled with his children, whom he had alienated so many years before. All five of his children have been involved with the Brownsville Revival. Even the Iranian boyfriend of one of his daughters was saved at the Brownsville altar.

As the power of God was going through her family like a tornado, JoAnn was undergoing her own transformation. Mary Kay

Cosmetics had been her life, but God made it clear that His will was for her to work with her husband. She quit her one-hundred-thousand-dollar-a-year job with Mary Kay.

"Now I finally know how JoAnn put up with me all those years," Robert says today, now that he knows how the power of God gives believers the grace to endure all kinds of grief—even the kind he caused.

As for that Gulf Coast condo that Robert was so intent on purchasing? Eventually, he did buy one—in Pensacola, so he could be closer to the Brownsville church. He even opened a branch office of his business there.

Meanwhile, the church was busier than ever with one of its new ventures, something of a business itself.

12

"WE WILL RIDE"

THE UNOFFICIAL RALLYING cry of the Brownsville Revival spawned a mini-industry of its own within the church.

"We Will Ride!"—the title of a song that has become synonymous with the Pensacola Outpouring—shows up on T-shirts and bumper stickers throughout the city. And when the design permits, that slogan includes a line from the song—"Yes, Lord, we will ride with You!"

One has to wonder how the uninitiated

interpret those words. But it's of little conse-
quence to those who buy the CDs and
cassettes. They're actually hoping that
people will ask what it means, just so they
can take advantage of a natural opportunity
to tell them about Brownsville and invite
them to the church.

What the song means is just what the
people of Brownsville Assembly of God
have been saying to the Lord for years: Yes.
Yes, we will fight along with the army of
heaven; we will ride with You into battle.
The vision the songs presents is one of Jesus
holding a sword, riding a white horse across
the country, and calling out for people who
will ride with Him into battle.

In all, four different CDs featuring praise
and worship songs from Brownsville—two
produced by the church, one by Vineyard
Music and one by Hosanna! Music—have
been released since the outbreak of revival.
The Vineyard release became one of Christian
music's top-selling CDs in the spring of
1997.

Like other revival hot-spots such as
Toronto, Pasadena, Sunderland, and London,
the move of God at Brownsville has its own

musical flavor—praise and worship with a Southern twang. Worship leader Lindell Cooley, who was hired as minister of music just a few weeks before revival broke out, set the tone early on, using his gift as a "prophetic musician"—one who follows the leading of the Holy Spirit in his worship style—to give Brownsville its distinctive emphasis on songs of repentance and salvation.

He also brought with him a wealth of experience that served him well when revival broke out. Before coming to Brownsville, he served as director of music at Christ Church in Nashville, the home church of many nationally known Christian musicians, including Naomi Judd, and a host of record industry insiders. He's worked with Bill Gaither, Dolly Parton, Garth Brooks, Larry Gatlin, Ricky Van Shelton, Cindy Morgan, and a host of other gospel music singers. Why he ended up in Pensacola ("the last place" he ever thought he'd live) would be something of a mystery if revival hadn't broken out.

Now, not even Cooley wonders why anymore. He's there to follow God and lead the people, in that order. And at nearly every service, Cooley does lead the congregation—especially in singing "We Will Ride."

Sharing the musical spotlight with Cooley is Charity James, who was a fifteen-year-old high school student at the time revival broke out. Her impact on Brownsville and the revival has been immeasurable. Her rendition of an old Pentecostal Holiness hymn, "Run to the Mercy Seat," not only mesmerizes the crowds at Brownsville but also her recording of the hymn reportedly has the same effect on listeners who have never set foot on Florida soil.

The haunting anthem, which urges sinners to find refuge in Jesus, seems to almost pull people to the altar. One night, a drug dealer from Hattiesburg, Mississippi, came to the Brownsville church by accident and ended up at the altar after Charity sang. Several weeks later, he was baptized. He and countless others credit "Run to the Mercy Seat"—and Charity's heartfelt vocal style—with creating the precise tug on their spirit that it would take to get them to the altar.

CDs featuring the worship music are a popular purchase among visitors eager to take a piece of Brownsville back to their own churches. The Brownsville songs have cropped up in the praise and worship roster of music ministers across the country and now around the world.

Visitors also sport buttons bearing the words "More, Lord!"—the worldwide rallying cry that the Toronto Blessing lent to the renewal.

Then there are the sales of thousands of video and cassette tapes of revival services and conferences and the videotape of Alison Ward's testimony; it's not unusual for a thousand tapes of the night's service to be sold even before Hill even finishes his altar call. It's apparent that this church can look like a business at times.

But don't expect this "business" to behave like any other—when it became apparent that hundreds of bootleg copies of the Alison Ward tape were in circulation, Hill's comment exposed his business sense. "That's fine with us," he shrugged. Anything to get the word out.

The church also sells kits for assembling prayer banners, in addition to photos of the banners and a manual explaining how to use them. And that, the church hopes, will get other congregations excited about the power of persistent, disciplined prayer. After all, that's what they believe started this whole revival rolling and what has kept it rolling for two years.

At Brownsville Assembly of God, it all comes back to prayer.

13

THE PRAYING PASTOR

THE MAN WHO BROUGHT Steve Hill to Pensacola after suffering one of the greatest losses of his life knew from an early age that he would be a preacher. There was simply never any doubt.

John Kilpatrick, pastor of Brownsville Assembly of God since 1982, was called to preach when he was only fourteen. As it turned out, he was in the perfect place to train for his future; his pastor in Columbus, Georgia, recognized the call of God on his life and immediately began training him for the ministry. As Kilpatrick will tell you, that training has served him well in these days of revival.

His pastor taught him that his success as a minister depended on the quality of his prayer life. And it was the quality of his prayer life, and that of his church, that laid the groundwork for the Brownsville Revival.

"During the past few years [before revival] we had gotten away from Pentecostal experiences and into sensationalism," Pastor John Kilpatrick says. "It caused us to become disoriented. We were searching for something that was real."

In 1988 Pastor Kilpatrick shifted the focus of his life to prayer. That began a special and intimate journey with God, as the Lord taught John Kilpatrick deeper and deeper lessons about the nature of prayer. He began to incorporate fasting into his prayer routine as well, further deepening the well of wisdom God was forming in his spirit.

All through the early nineties, Kilpatrick led his church in a growing awakening into the power of prayer. By 1993 regular, systematic prayer was firmly entrenched in the congregation's worship routine.

Then, in February of 1995 Kilpatrick's wife, Brenda—who knew at an early age she was called to be a pastor's wife—traveled to the renewal hotbed at the time, Toronto Airport Christian Fellowship. A woman she did not know approached her during one of the renewal services there and asked, "May I touch you?"

Brenda complied.

"She felt fire come on top of her head," Kilpatrick says. "Then she fell and stayed on the floor for an hour. She felt so relaxed."

When Brenda told John about that experience, his heart lit up.

"I ignited," he says.

He witnessed such a radical change in his wife that he hardly knew what to think. One day when they were having lunch at a local restaurant, Brenda was glowing with the presence of God—and John started crying. Brenda laughed. The more John cried, the more Brenda laughed. After twenty-seven years of marriage, John wasn't quite sure what was going on. He only knew that the strange behavior they were both exhibiting had somehow made them hungry for more of God and more of His Word.

And make no mistake about it, Pastor Kilpatrick loves the Word of God. It was to the Word of God that Kilpatrick turned when the Holy Spirit spoke to him about sending a helper, and that's when he read Ecclesiastes 4:9, the verse that spoke so personally to him about the rewards of companionship.

That verse was never more real than it was on that Father's Day morning, the day when a grieving son called on his friend to take his place in the pulpit. Especially when he realized the impact that filling-in would later have.

"Most pastors would deeply appreciate God sending them someone to help them in such a way," Kilpatrick told *Charisma.* "Many men of God have been put up on a pedestal, carrying the whole load on their shoulders while the devil has been picking them off like crazy.

"But when a pastor bonds together with an evangelist, and they are moving together in their own gifts, that's a pretty tough team to pull down."

The impact of the pastor-evangelist team is being felt thousands of miles away in the city of Sunderland, England. At a 1996 conference in Kentucky, Kilpatrick met

Sunderland pastor Ken Gott and prophesied over him that God would send someone to help him with the explosive renewal there.

That evangelist turned out to be J John, England's best known evangelist—so much so that he's called the "British Billy Graham." J John conducts evangelistic services in Sunderland every Friday night. And once again the pastor-evangelist team has proven to be a pretty tough one to pull down—even in Sunderland, where lives are at risk for sharing the gospel.

Back in Pensacola, Kilpatrick admits that revival, as glorious as it is, is not without its disappointments. A self-described people person, Kilpatrick has been forced to give up much of the day-to-day work of running the church. With the much-needed addition of more staff, the pastor has become a manager—"which I hate," he says.

"But we still have the normal routine," he adds. "I still marry people and bury people. I want our people to know that their pastor is still there—that there is normalcy."

There's not a whole lot of normalcy left for the people at Brownsville Assembly of God. Church members even are issued tickets to renewal services just so they can be sure they get a seat.

Like the lives of those impacted by the apostles in the first century, their lives have been turned upside down.

14

BROWNSVILLE TODAY

S INCE JUNE OF 1995 some 1.5 million people have visited the unassuming church on Desoto Street in Pensacola. Nearly one hundred thousand people have been saved, and the tally is likely to go higher. Countless backslidden Christians have found their first love again. Hundreds of others have been healed and delivered.

But what has all this meant to the people of Brownsville Assembly of God?

To be sure, the cost of revival has been high. Not just the emotional and physical cost but the financial cost as well.

The church's monthly security bill runs ten thousand dollars. Each night that there's a service, security guards patrol a half-mile radius in which visitors' cars are parked. With services often lasting until three o'clock in the morning, extra security is viewed as a necessity, not a luxury.

The nightly water bill runs more than $150; toilet paper is delivered by the truck-load. And the church hired nursery workers, because the staff did not feel they could expect church members to volunteer that much time. That bill once topped out at four thousand dollars a month.

Manpower needs are high as well. The church has trained nearly four hundred prayer counselors and seventy-five ushers. Twenty deacons serve the church.

And then there's the toll the revival has taken on the physical facilities.

"Our building has taken a trampling," admits Pastor John Kilpatrick.

During the first year after revival broke out, the church was forced to buy adjoining property to accommodate the growth. Construction of a five thousand-seat multi-purpose building to be known as the Family Life Center began in the spring of 1997.

"The sanctuary would fill up in sixty seconds [for revival services]," Steve Hill said. "But we didn't want to move the revival to the civic center." The only alternative was to build.

The revival has attracted so many pastors and leaders from the United States and around the world that the church now hosts semi-annual pastors' conferences. When the first conference drew nearly seven hundred pastors only five months after the revival started, Kilpatrick was amazed. Now, the pastors' conference draws more than two thousand leaders.

Through it all, prayer continues to be the primary focus of the church. The Tuesday night prayer meeting is open to everyone, though participants from other denominations are encouraged to get permission from their pastors. Attendance can run as high as one thousand at the prayer meeting; some people drive a hundred miles or more just to attend.

And every night, a team of intercessors meets for prayer, joined by pastors and lay people from other churches. Kilpatrick has no intention of eliminating the focus on prayer. "If we stopped the prayer meetings, I know this move of God would grind to a halt," he said.

And without prayer, there's no telling what would happen to the members of Brownsville. For them, revival of this magnitude translates into a huge sacrifice.

"Our members get off work at five or six P.M., and by the time they get to the church, there are two thousand people waiting to get inside," said Kilpatrick. "Members of Brownsville Assembly can't even get in their own church. I try to help my congregation feel good on a continual basis about what God is doing here."

One thing that could stop this revival dead in its tracks is exhaustion. Charles Finney recognized this as well, Hill said.

"You can work yourself to death, and it doesn't glorify God," said Hill. "Revival will rearrange your schedule, but after you have become acclimated to it, you've got to see how you can function."

For Hill, that means a conscious effort to pace himself, napping in the afternoon whenever possible. For Kilpatrick, it means taking every other Monday off, hiring extra staff, delegating jobs, and reminding himself that he doesn't have to be at the church all the time. "That does relieve some of the pressure," he said—admitting, though, that when he misses a revival service, "my evening seems empty and unproductive. I just want to be back in church because it's so wonderful."

And for both men, the best medicine for fatigue is another healthy dose of prayer. Hill never steps into the pulpit without the intercessory team praying over him first. That, he said, goes a long way toward refreshing him each night.

"You can't do it all," he said. "Some things have to fall by the wayside. As much as I would love to sit down and dine with people, I don't do that because it's so time-consuming. I keep a low profile."

Mealtimes are spent with his wife, Jeri, and their three young children, Ryan, Shelby, and Kelsey Noel. Those are four people he has no intention of sacrificing at the altar of revival. "I don't want to win the world and lose my own family," said Hill.

Still, his family attends the revival every night. They wouldn't miss it.

"I liken revival to war," said Hill. "A soldier trains for war, but when war breaks out the training is over. It's time to fight. I'll fight until the battle is over each night."

Like war, revival takes its toll, Hill said.

"Revival is expensive—financially, physically, emotionally, and spiritually. You must have a real hunger for God to move."

And to date, that hunger shows no sign of being satisfied.

15

THE BEST IS
YET TO COME

ONE THING ABOUT this revival that John Kilpatrick makes clear is that even though this move of God may be known as the Brownsville Revival, it's not a Brownsville thing. "This is a God thing," Kilpatrick says, and you know he means it.

That's one aspect of this revival that will never change, as far as John Kilpatrick and Stephen Hill are concerned. While it may have started in one church, through the preaching of one man, the two main figures in this revival are determined that the focus will always be on Jesus, never on a man or a church. Stephen Hill is so intent on that that he declined to appear on the cover of *Charisma*.

"We try to stay out of the picture as much as possible," Hill told *Charisma*. "The revival is about Jesus. It's not about a man."

And he intends to remain under the leadership of John Kilpatrick for as long as God wants him to. Hill sees his submission to Kilpatrick as one of the keys to the continuation of the Brownsville Revival.

"We discuss everything, and we make a lot of decisions together," Kilpatrick explains. "I'm not going to do anything that would disturb his authority."

The future of the revival—or just as importantly, the future of those touched by it—also lies in Brownsville's commitment to the continued discipleship of new converts. Hundreds of newborn Christians take the church's discipleship class; countless others attend similar classes in churches throughout the city.

"But the main thing that disciples the converts is the revival itself," said Hill. "People get saved, and six months later you'd think they've known the Lord for years.

"Some came to the revival not knowing anything about the Lord; they shook under the power, fell to the ground, and had a great experience. You don't need that all the time, but all of us need to have a genuine encounter with God. And some folks who were initially touched in a physical way have now moved to spiritual depth. They're in the intercessory prayer room every night, weeping for those who will be saved that night."

A second factor that Hill believes will go a long way toward keeping the flames of revival burning is simply allowing God to control the burn.

"Many of our denominations were born in the fire," Hill points out. "John Wesley asked the Lord to send a revival without any defects, but he added that if that's not possible, then send a revival with defects."

It's the defects of revival that often result in the revival being quenched—not by the problems they create but by control-oriented leaders who try to act as God's deputies, Hill believes.

"Revival will have its problems," he said. "You can go to any meeting anywhere and see flesh, if that's what you're looking for. I don't go to these meetings looking for flesh; I go looking for God."

By Hill's estimate, 95 percent of what goes on in a typical Brownsville meeting is part of a sovereign move of God.

"Am I going to concentrate on the 5 percent? No. You deal with the important situations, but you let God control the revival."

Hill has no doubt that with God in control, American believers will eventually see such miracles as the raising of the dead—a phenomenon reported primarily among third-world believers.

"This revival has given me hope for America," said Hill. "I believe that over the next few years, this entire country will be set ablaze by the power of God.

"We're seeing miraculous healings, cancerous tumors disappear, drugs addicts immediately delivered, and the demon-possessed set free. Everyone who has been touched by this revival will agree that it's like a cold slap in the face. It's a wake-up call out of a spiritual slumber."

"Every true outpouring has one focus: to

reach the lost," said Dan Livingston, pastor of First Assembly of God, who believes the future of the revival depends on maintaining its focus on salvations.

"When we focus on the church, that's the end of it. And it could be easy to get focused on the marketing of this thing. My prayer is, 'Please God, don't let me mess this up.'"

"God's people are worn-out, stressed-out, burned-out," John Kilpatrick said. "This move of the Holy Spirit happening around the world is God reviving His people."

No matter what happens to this revival in the coming years, one of the countless people who has been changed forever is John Kilpatrick himself. Television has lost its appeal; after experiencing the holy environment of revival, there's not a whole lot of television he feels comfortable watching anymore. His compassion for the lost translates into a whole new perspective on sinners; now he sees them as souls to be saved.

Today, when Kilpatrick drives by the church at mid-afternoon and sees hundreds of people outside waiting to get in to the evening service, the pastor has to turn his head and look away. It's a humbling experience for him to see the power of God move so mightily at his church. It's also humbling to see well-known pastors from around the country waiting in line for three hours in the hot Florida sun—"getting sweaty with the rest of the people"—rather than seeking preferential treatment.

"For God to lay His hand on our church to this magnitude has so humbled me," he told *Charisma*. "I've never seen such spiritual hunger. I gear my prayer life and my sermons toward that spiritual hunger.

"If this revival came to a grinding halt, I could never go back to the way things were. I'll never be the same again. Never."

*The weekly schedule for Brownsville Assembly
of God is as follows:*

Sunday

- Sunday school: 8:45 A.M.
- Nursery church: 9:00 A.M.
- Worship service: 10:00 A.M.
- Children's church: 10:00 A.M.

Monday

- No service is scheduled.

Tuesday

- Prayer meeting: 7:00 P.M.

Wednesday—Friday

- Revival services held nightly beginning at 7:00 P.M. Baptismal services are held during the Friday evening service.
- Wednesday nights: Royal Rangers and Missionettes (ages 4–14).
- Thursday nights: Youth service in the chapel (ages 12–18).

Saturday

- Revival service begins at 6:00 P.M.